HOW STEEL IS MADE

I WONDER
HOW STEEL IS MADE

Neil Curtis and Peter Greenland

Lerner Publications Company • Minneapolis

This edition published 1992
by Lerner Publications Company
241 First Avenue North
Minneapolis, Minnesota 55401 USA

Original edition published in 1990 by Heinemann Educational
Books Ltd., Halley Court, Jordan Hill, Oxford OX28EJ England
Copyright © 1990 by Heinemann Educational Books Ltd.

Library of Congress Cataloging-in-Publication Data

Curtis, Neil.
    How steel is made / Neil Curtis and Peter Greenland.
        p.   cm.—(I wonder)
    Originally published: Oxford, England : Heinemann
Educational Books, 1990.
    Summary: Describes how steel is made, beginning in an iron
ore mine and ending at a steel mill.
    ISBN 0-8225-2378-7
    1. Steel—Juvenile literature. [1. Steel.] I. Greenland, Peter. II.
Title. III. Series: Curtis, Neil. I wonder.
TN732.C87 1992
669.142—dc20   91-24209
                                                              CIP
                                                              AC

Manufactured in the United States of America.

1 2 3 4 5 6 7 8 9 10 01 00 99 98 97 96 95 94 93 92

Steel is a strong metal.
Airplanes, cars, and buildings are made from steel.

Steel is a kind of iron.
Iron comes from rocks called iron ore,
which miners dig from the ground.

Ships take the iron ore to factories,
where it will be made into steel.
Giant cranes unload the iron ore from the ships.

A factory that makes steel is called a steel mill.

At the mill, workers make coke.
Coke is a fuel that will melt the iron.
It is made by heating coal in large ovens.

The coke and iron ore are mixed together
in a large furnace.
Then the workers add limestone,
a kind of chalky rock.

Very hot air is blasted into
the bottom of the furnace.
This hot air makes the coke burn.
Inside the furnace, the temperature rises
above 3,000° F (1,600° C).

The burning coke melts the iron ore.
A pool of hot, liquid iron forms at the bottom
of the furnace.

Other parts of the ore melt with the limestone.
This mixture is called slag.
The slag floats on top of the pool of iron
and is drained off.

Then the slag is poured into huge containers
that are carried on railroad cars.

Some of the slag will be used to make cement.
Most of it will be thrown away.

If the liquid iron were cooled,
it would become solid.
Solid iron is hard, but it breaks easily.
People used to make tools out of iron.

In steel-making, the liquid iron is not allowed to cool.
It goes into a different kind of furnace
where it is kept hot.

Some steel is made in an electric furnace.

Steel can also be made in a furnace that
is heated with oxygen.
The heat in the furnaces removes a chemical
called carbon from the iron.

As the carbon is removed from the iron,
the iron turns into steel.
A worker takes a sample of the liquid steel
from the furnace.

The worker tests the sample to make sure
the steel will be strong.

Liquid steel may be poured into a mold to cool. Blocks of molded steel are called ingots.

Ingots are used to make steel slabs.
First the ingots must be heated again.
Then special machines with rollers
flatten the steel into slabs.

Liquid steel may also be shaped into bars.
These long bars are called blooms.

Hot blooms and slabs
are cut into pieces with torches.

Steel is then rolled into thin sheets
or shaped with powerful hammers.
Steel can be used to make tools, bicycles,
cars, and machines.

24